Two Minutes of Light

Two Minutes of Light

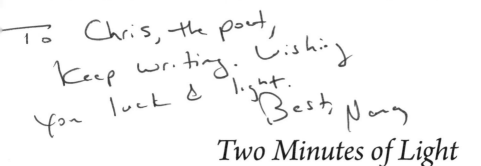

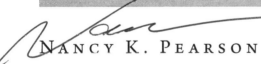

NANCY K. PEARSON

PERUGIA PRESS
FLORENCE, MASSACHUSETTS
2008

Perugia Press extends deeply felt thanks to the many individuals whose generosity made the publication of *Two Minutes of Light* possible. Perugia Press is a tax-exempt, nonprofit 501(c)(3) corporation publishing first and second books by women. To make a tax-deductible donation, please contact us directly or visit our Web site.

Cover image is *Traffic Light,* oil on canvas, by Damien Baumgartner, used with permission of the artist and the owner. See www.libbyedwardsgalleries.com.

Author photo by Elizabeth Winston.

Book Design by Jeff Potter and Susan Kan.

The fact about suicide in "Two Worlds" comes from "The British Gas Suicide Story and Its Criminological Implications," by Ronald V. Clarke and Pat Mayhew from *Crime and Justice,* Vol. 10, 1988, pp. 79–116. Accounting for more than forty percent of suicides in 1963, suicide by domestic gas was all but eliminated by 1975, after the progressive removal of carbon monoxide from the public gas supply. Few of those prevented from using gas appear to have found some other way of killing themselves.

Library of Congress Cataloging-in-Publication Data

Pearson, Nancy K., 1969-

   Two minutes of light / Nancy K. Pearson.

      p. cm.

   ISBN 978-0-9794582-1-7

   I. Title.

   PS3616.E257T96 2008

   811'.6--dc22

                                        2008017066

Perugia Press

P.O. Box 60364

Florence, MA 01062

info@perugiapress.com

http://www.perugiapress.com

In memory of
Nancy DeVriendt

For Elizabeth
with love

Contents

There came a time when the risk to remain tight in the bud was more painful than the risk it took to blossom.

— *Anaïs Nin*

Cyclic

The fiddler crabs are barn-raising
their sink holes in the sand.
All morning, the leggy low tide calls
allemandes left and right.

I am twelve.   My father and his four girls
are fishing the yellow marsh.   It is easy —
reeling in small loaves
of sunlight, before the winter

I began slicing my wrists like fruit,
before I spent my Medicaid checks on crack,
before I demanded the world recognize
my suffering.

My father baits our hooks, forgetting his own.
We are four girls fishing
before high tide,
before the sea water surrounds us

like a horse gallop,
how it explodes a field of birds —
black wings breaking a sure hunk of sky
into a thousand parts.

ELSEWHERE

That winter the wrapper leaves fell off every head of lettuce.
The cutters and packers worked all day, stooping
between the frozen rows, rising creaked and creased
in the gray sunlight, whole families bent at the waist,
broken midrib and pink-veined, the lettuce,
the slick lemon and orange trees smoking,
diesel smudge pots burning all night, steamed-up vans patrolling
the cities for homeless dogs or men. The benches
were empty. The blankets ran out. Trains derailed
on Chickamauga lake. My brother drove his new Toyota in circles,
Holiday Bowl closed early. Trees pulled open shingles, seeds scooted.
In the bathroom my mother stood over me squirting Nice 'n Easy
in a line across my darkening part, her eyeliner wet, the yellow
gone from everything now, someone's son or daughter
still bending in the crunchy loam,
flood lights rowing over the bald heads of lettuce,
over and over, knife through root, the cold unlucky
miles of heavy lemons dropping elsewhere.

SHUCKING

As a child, I lost two sides of a mouth.   A shucked space
where the tub wrecked one summer night

replaced my front teeth with a void
that soon forgot which loss it mapped.

Rice-like, they dallied then sank.
In the meat-red spit, the soap circled.

My mother, running for the car; my father still fishing
in the lukewarm water — this, the last year of a marriage.

All night my small mouth raked without its razor tines.
I do not remember this, or my father weeping afterwards in the tender field,

pea-picking in the star-sprouted evening,
life's extractions piled green and sea-surrounding.

Later that night, a strange wind off-hitched every pod and downed.
By morning, only muscle scars where the fruit once hinged.

SILVER BIMBO MUD FLAP SONG

lord, my one leg is sinking
and the sister leg wants out of the litter of reeds —
that church of crawl,
        and step
       and run

evening blows through my stepfather's trailer —
a pulley of cool,
my spread toes tuck under my belly

      (straw-runged cattail bent
      bird-legged little ol' girl
      in the dictionary of dirt)

hwy 6 on the left,
silver bimbo mud flaps humming
outside the twin bed scree

the din of his beating heart,
acorns falling on the roof,
someone play me a moon suite

leafless stars, thin mattress,
he rolls me over
    (splash of freckles)

and over
    (splash of freckles)
all things finally fall,
acorns, his limp hand from the edge,
    (dangle sound)

my one leg pinned under his,

crabs at the toes
silver mud eels
crabs at the toes

CAT

How he dragged himself across a two-lane interstate,
through the tussle of marsh, past a coyote den littered
with fifty or so cat collars and twisted himself under the clowning
hydrangea bush, how the wind unplugged
the sand dunes, grain by grain, all day, how even the ponds lifted a little,
unanchoring from the pink cords of lilies, the tacked down pods of rain,
everything rose up to meet him.
I was crossing the street in a hurry, late
for bussing tables, green bracts floated from a stem.   I did not hear
his small mew darting up, a heart minnowing forward,
how both hip bones closed toward the center
where a wheel crushed earlier that morning,
wings folded around the organs, a songbird without hinges,
how he could not stand, how could he
and yet, later, how I found him on the bed curled beside the sleeping dog.

At the Boneyard

Searching for mud flaps for an old bicycle,
the bay beside it throwing out crab traps,
the sooty power plant behind it
smearing the sky like a snag
in a pair of white tights she can never keep in place,
always sliding from the middle of her,
someone's hands madly searching
the boneyard, the wet places.
Nothing could make her happier now thinking
about those red crabs in the bay escaping
through the broken wires and wheeling
with their pairs of broken fenders out to sea.

SKIMMERS

For now, my stepfather
is content, throwing
stones at the pond skimmers.

The water quickly knits
a flush tunnel.   The bugs go under.
I am a mechanical creature

following his lead.
We took the old road
to this brackish hole.

The good road,
the one with hay over the mud,
was taken by the faithful.

I tell him I am falling.
He tells me I am walking
in the woods.   The punk

misfit sleeps on a log,
the four wheelers have deflated
the silent float of weeds.

Van Camps cans, Trojan wrappers,
the plucked blackberry carry the sound
of yellow teeth.   The firs

at the pond know when
to free their leaves: lie down
under here, love.

Here is a teeth grove.
He smiles, legs straddled
over me.

Over there now,
the Jesus bugs sail free.

Track Star

Where lightning once entered —
now a pattern of fern leaves.   When it was clear

there was no cure, you took off,
the hunt and peck of rain on the bleachers,

small cages of neon flickering.   Like you had all those years
you ran around the red crumb rubber

to the dead straightaway where the digital motors thumb,
where the great silver planets of finishers fall.

From the stands, a shallow boosterism of crows.
And afterwards, your bent body — neither blown apart

nor snapped back together.   The joints,
the muscles not balanced,

not totaled.   The losses: one kill frost like another.
We shrivel from ice or thirst.

Across the soccer field — little bombs of milkweed,
their sweet, white slow-motion explosion before winter.

NEEDLE GIRLS

It is August.   A girl watches the rain
double whammy on the tarp-wide

squash leaves.   Wire-haired vegetables flesh out
into the nineteenth century.   The rain ends.

Galaxies of bees waggle over Denmark.
A young girl pushes a prayer book

embedded with a needle into her chest.   Summer
flattens.   Hills grow inward.

What they took from her:
shoe nails, glass, 217 needles.   What was missing

bore under her skin.   All across Europe, these needle girls.
The world is not in conflict,

not now.   Two centuries later, an ER doctor,
thread in hand, holds a girl's sliced wrist in the air, and says

this way, pointing with his pen,
next time, cut them both, this way.

From the Motel-by-the-Hour

1.

I lost my straight shooter, a sawed-off sparkplug
somewhere in a cheap motel.
All night, I search for pipes —
tire gauge, rusted beer can, hollowed-out cigar.

Months ago, I drove across the country,
left my home in the wet hills of Tennessee,
found the unfolding pageant of billboards,
squashed possum, tugboat clouds,

hills repeating hills, freewheeling leaves going insane.
Thought I could drive my past away.
I'm here now and hunched over,
searching for a boost.

Behind me, that red suspension bridge
sinks into the deep fog,
leaves this bright world behind
for another.

2.

Strung out, Silva and I need a bump.
The wind, spring-loaded and snap-buckling
through the cypress, creeps in,
splinters the stash thin across the motel floor.

We are crawling and picking through the carpet.
Silva says, *stop pushing my head down, Reggie,*
my knees got seeds mashed in them.
Night is a rerun rerun.   Fight over a pebble high:

that long five minutes.   Reggie watches us buck and kiss.
Silva on the floor again.   *(Stop pushing my head down, Reg.)*
The shag hooks her silver hoop —
ear snagged and hanging off

like old fish bait.   Stuck down there,
someone just cover her up.

3.

Silva's in the hallway bathroom.
She's clawing up her face again.
Reggie is laughing real loud,
Silva, you a goddamn puller now.

I don't want to see her face,
her skin peeling off her cheekbone,
pores torn bigger, a face on hinges.
I'm high and want to feel her tits,

put my mouth on her hard nipples.
Fuck Reggie's laughing.
I don't want to think about the scabs,
the other night, me with my panties

twisted up in my crack,
biting down hard on her,
getting up quickly
with blood in my teeth,

peeing in the free-standing sink
in the middle of the room,
my thighs shaking
like the hind legs of a dog.

4.

I carry my index finger in my hand.
I cut it off earlier, straight through the bone
just to see if I could.
I cup it warily

as if the bone could beat free,
a broken bird with flittering wings.
The hospital is down Fillmore Street.
I walk with a spring, kick an old donut

eaten out by ants, shoot it right into a drain.
God, I'm good.   Good god.

5.

Jimmy has a tattoo of a beet on his left arm.
People often mistake it for an organ.
I like the idea of someone who loves taproots so much
he'll suffer an afternoon under the needle

for a swollen red stem.   That Jimmy.
I want to see him again and the other gay boys from *Greens*
with their clean haircuts and brilliant skin.
Tonight, Silva yells, *honey git me my wig* and I do.

Her left arm is swollen up like an udder,
her silver rings cut deep into her ashen skin.
Somewhere, young Jimmy chops onions and parsley,
his tuber tattoo beating like a purplish heart.

6.

Silva runs down the hallway after Reggie
leaving with the stash.   Her feet sound like stakes
shoving into the floor.
Silva, eat something for god's sake,

I yell and don't know why I'm yelling this right now.
I think of an old cow, wobbling on thin ankles,
spine like a curtain rod, skin in the breeze.
Baby, she says later, throat full of smoke,
open your mouth.

The sweet crack flows into me.
I touch her teeth with my tongue.
They are cow-licked and scoured out.
Baby, she says, *you've got it bad.*

SONNET TO SLEEP

While you drive down an interstate
with the thousand bug-eyed hum of June,
I line pinched fleas on a bedside plate.
In the alcohol jar, tiny insects weigh the moon

carving up the locust trees berthing
night.   Hollow freights of dogs spill
across the suburbs.   Nothing
is unbearable without you, still

all night I count blue sheep stalled
in lorries moving across the bending
plains.   They lick the metal walls
desperate with thirst on their never-ending

slaughter journey.   The dog folds
into herself like a take-out box junk-yarded.
The oily pattern, the untold
story we leave on everything discarded

now falls on some remote highway shrinking
while sheep die crocus-tongued and blinking.

At the Colorado State Psychiatric Hospital

No one around here knows the difference
between a return of reason and a certain cunning.   I'm playing

dead, floating with my head down.
My hair dangles like kelp sucked toward the drain.

All day I follow the anvil clouds, the great sky capacitors
throwing hot wire into the sea.

Later, a guard shouts: *Everybody out of the water.*
Now dripping on the sand,

such easy humility, these things,
waiting it out, the decisions made for you, following

the whistles: Circle up, confess, turn in sharp items.
I watch the endless buildup, every day

a puddle, a great lake escapes and rises
so high above me.

So a New Coat Will Grow

The tree next to the Sav-On sheds
a thousand yellow leaves: litter of glow
and crunch.   Street lights devour
the early bird buffet of stars.

Here I am again without you.   Ice cubes unscrewing
to the bottom.   The woman outside my apartment
is combing the grass.   All evening,
with a big-toothed comb,

she scrapes her collie's blue fur from the yard.
Between the rocky piles of shit,
this pulling, brown grasses,
blue hair, piles of shit.

The street lamp waters her and I down
another drink.   Later, night knits a sleeve,
catches me fishing
your long hair from my drain.

Hiking the Appalachian Trail

for Robbie

1.

Early morning begins again at mile zero.
After moonset, before sunrise
the meteor storm —
buckshot,
    milk-spray   through a front tooth,
    one million seeds   in a field of strawberries.
not another like this for seventy-five years.

2.

I hear my heart in my ears as we climb.
The clouds grow infinite and arabesque.
I ask, *when will we reach Clingman's Dome?*
Later, in silence, we eat dried apples and sesame mix.
Finally, the long green fir tunnel
                    releases to a bald opening.

3.

On a clear spring night, he pulled himself up
onto the bent leg of Robert E. Lee,
dew on his gloves, his boots steady,
he reached for the outstretched arm of the statue,
hoisting his young body higher.
The others sipped whiskey from a flask   (it was a late night bar bet)

      and cheered higher.

The bare tulip trees grew   smaller
in the thin diet   of moon.

4.

We have been climbing the trail all day.
The tunnel of birch,
and everywhere
        the brown leaf parodies itself,
          the brown leaf parodies
            the brown leaf.

5.

When Robbie fell, his temple hit the marble block.
Under the bronze boots of General E. Lee
he laughed — *that was a stupid thing*
       to do-o.
When his eyes closed shut
his mouth opened to an O,
the shape of the second
after
       do
folded inward
forever.

6.

You boil water on the Whisper Light stove.
I open the noodles.
Tomorrow and the next,
        months funneling through ice puddle, crocus,
                rhododendron, azalea and black fly,
we will wake only to walk.

7.

Maybe we should have
                        waited longer.
Sometimes, doesn't the body surprise
        even the sure flat line of the monitor?
His swollen brain was:
pushing, Mr. and Mrs. Martin, on the coronal suture,
        which holds the left and right parietal plates together.
The medulla functioning
for what was once —
        skip a stone over the James River —
                wince and the zing of his first olive —
                        back flip from the yellow dock —
kiss her here by the old hunting shed —
                        hold the line tight with the biggest bass ever —
                                and ah, reeling it in.
A shunt.   A rotating bed.   His body packed in ice.
His heart the constant sound of a car alarm
        in a street of purple light.
When we finally said: turn it all off, yes,   turn him off,

I remember thinking:
    his heart will keep beating.

8.

The meteors again,
    a gap in the pines.
I feel the brace of my boots
    and rumble a cough through the silence.
We are still climbing
    and I am not comforted by the trail guide:
for seventy miles the trail climbs steeper into the Smokies.
Fist of wet socks, pine needles, pine needles,
palaver of wind
                go on.

JEWELWEED

Trajectories blast off,
arc and down a hundred times a day.
Oddments of seedpods, the neap tide of wind,
the recurved tails of jewelweed everywhere.

It was a Tuesday.   I was drinking vodka
before noon.   Outside the heat was a thorn,
the porch shade nervous, the remains of the lilies —
pitchforks.

Days started like this:
You couldn't find a sock to wear with your suit.
I couldn't find it for you.   I couldn't hold a job.

A gnat suspended the breeze and arced for my glass.
I thought of all my landings, my fight with medium,
my quick ignitions and even faster snuffs.

The sun makes a beeline for my ice.
I pour another.   I used to have a seedcase of dreams —
sainthood, the Olympics, an honest answer,
folded laundry.

When ripe, a pod of jewelweed explodes
under the slightest disturbance.
Trap one in your fingertips,
unzip.

TWO WORLDS

Between 1963 and 1975 the number of suicides in England showed
a sudden, unexpected decline. This appears to be the result of the
progressive removal of carbon monoxide from the public gas supply.

If they built a barrier, we could still see those bell-lit sheep, the stars,
herding toward sea. If they built a barrier, the shrimp-toast fog

would still climb the sky no-handed. If they a built a railing,
a sleek-curved flowing arched fence, a suicide barrier,

still we could watch the city throw its lights overboard
into the bay, the wind surfers sliding around

like dry leaves. If they built a higher fence, every ten days
a man, a woman would walk back

across the Golden Gate Bridge alive,
suddenly alive. Looking down, we stand

between two worlds. A young man jumps
from twenty-five stories. He lives to tell you this:

the suicidal aren't meant to die. When he hit the water,
his backbones tangled like water root. He could not swim

broken. *A seal*, he says, *I swear there was a seal.*
By what small margins do we survive?

Under the bridge tonight, a smoke flare rises
from the black water, another narrow ghost crossed over.

WINTER SOLSTICE, 4TH FLOOR

The nurse's flashlight peels back
a second of my shallow sleep
through the door like a thread
of digital yellow carpet

pulled through a latch hook
every fifteen minutes.   I wake
at thirty and feel old, color-leached,

a rowboat rooted with sea grass.
The back of my knee
sucks on a plastic hospital sheet.

The woman in the next bed
drags an eraser over her wrists
again and again, her skin like sawdust.
One summer my childhood

dog was eaten alive by fleas.
In the wire cage where she lived,
I found her curled in her own pink pulp.

I move to the cigarette lounge,
one white fish in a smokebowl,
watch the large hand orbit an inch —

two minutes of light
is what we gain every day
after the solstice.   I hold on
to a small tangerine,

unwrap the orange collars
releasing the briefest hues.

The Halfway-to-Hell Club

I don't ask for forgiveness, not now, not ever.
I left the house early.   The day wore teeth.

Baby, I wanted to tell you the truth:
I lied when I said I was well.

Later, my shrink searched the streets.
The police called and you answered.

What they said was this: *Lady, go down to your basement.*
She's probably hanging there.

I imagine you, like an ironworker fallen and caught in a net
suspended high over the Golden Gate Strait,

you, stopping yourself abruptly
halfway down the basement steps —

Every Knee Bends

All summer I sleep on couches.
Popcorn, penny-eating things.

Sectionals divide and pull under.
A cat licks my eyebrows and I wake

with someone's fingernails between my toes.
The night I left you, I ran down a salt-dusted road.

The January sky pulled down its hoodoo of stars,
snow covered the tracks from our house.

Once, I felt secure —
we were in a tent and you asked,

what do you love?
The strange woods groaned.

It was cold.   I spooned from the silence:
Your leg on mine.

Tonight, I sleep on a love seat.
It folds me in two.   Once again,

I make a throne on what is lost.
A nickel finds my calf.

My toe picks a comb.
My knees ask my heart why it runs.

THE SIGN

on the hospital door says: No Flowers or Fruit.
Days before, my iron turned on High,
I wanted to be something

newly suffused, something becoming,
like a snake hiding in the skull of a wombat,
skin loosening around the lips,

then slowly forced back over the head,
neck and body, inside out.
Wheeled from post-op,

my burned arm covered
with skin from my thigh,
my new roommate tells me

how she learned to walk again
after her liver transplant,
falling on the way to the bathroom,

how she carried forty pounds
of fluid on her ninety-pound frame.
She tells me relearning

is a controlled falling.
I live my life wanting
anything vulnerable and vivid.

And this tiny woman lying beside me —
a wild lily could kill her.

Halfway to Flight

In early March, division and displacement
unlock an iris patch in a field of weeds.
One stroke of green carved out from the others
yields a summer.

I spent the decade adding:
years sitting in hospital admissions
rating lethality on a scale of one to ten,
arms all sliced up like pears,

nights spent piss drunk,
wetting someone's groovy sheets,
empty bottles, empty jobs —
still, my heart goes on dividing

its twisted yarn of blood.
The valves sing: knot here, snip there.
Cut from the soil, an iris aches like a bone.
I plant it in the yard, my single green wing.

Keep a Watch over My Mouth, Etc.

O lord keep the door of my lips —
it is too early for this power-tooled variation
on frame and rise, fence or wall, nail by nail a vine of drill,
chainsaw bloom of kickback, deck expansion,

pneumatic sunrise I am always
dreaming of toothful fish or gnawing stars
these are not good neighbors, the 4 AM synths,
the amplified skiffs, elsewhere and far, a lighthouse

breaks open the glassy nap of a lost sailor
or the town drunk, head now flashlight wonked,
or a woman waking in the donut ring of her skirt
she is not in her dorm, the fog outside

dripping and then spilling, she walks
with her pumps in one hand down a highway
it is too early for the bus, under the body count
headlines, I read about this, what happens next

before sunrise, before the door of my lips opens
in curse, in song for the constant drilling next door
I wake knowing where I am

Song for the Scars

It's so simple in the sunlight,
the hands move like birds,
pear-weight planets flying
into orbit.   They fish spoons
from the drain, weed sand
burrs from the dog.
The hands know the delicacy
of a moment: the formation of
a suture loop, picking meat from the bone.

The arms, they carry a weight.
The little blue pine just planted,
now carried for the curb,
dirt udder hanging.
The cocktail tray,
the spaghetti plates gliding around,
balance and serve and serve.
Heavy child.   Heavy wood.

My arms are a winter landfill —
wind-wrecked and spined,
small hills of white mattress bones.
In the dark night, a hand will destroy
what the arm bears —
the scars, they rise like wakes,
the white lines
of something heavy
passing.

CROCUS

For months now I am bleak and primitive.
The congregation of crows refutes
the resurrection of anything.

I sleep all day, drink all night.
I believe only in certainty of equations,
the curvature of space, words used merely for incantation.

This cold wind I sway in, this continual lent —
But wait, the first crocus
throws dirt.

I Still Cannot Touch Him

Driving south, the windshield wipers gut a bug,
greasy murder ballad,
the wet road spronged with possum.

Farther down, past the oxblood barns,
past Wild Bill's and the house of fire,
I know there is forgiveness.

The fervor of stagnation hums in a drain ditch.
An old man sets his traps,
dazed by the shimmering heat.

Way down a dirt road,
past the chickens pecking glass,
is a woman singing the Aqua Net blues.

And here, a front porch —
some bygones gone right beside
the old steel glider.

And behind the house, that horrible horse,
his speckled blue gums shining
through the barbed wire fence.

Sunset on Sequoyah

Across the gray water, darting in and out of shade, two girls ski.
They throw their bodies so far away from center like spinners on fly-lines,

reeling themselves back again and again under the hunky shadows
of the cooling towers.   On the bank, sandhill cranes slump.

The sky strips to its waist, the sun dipping behind Sequoyah Nuclear Plant.
Men punch out for the day, casting off hard hats for exhaustion.   At the bar,

I sweep the deck, push-broom shrimp shells, beer caps into the river.
I am thirty-two, divorced, living with my mother.   In front of me,

they appear, the two girls flinging their small arms up
into the air.   The ropes fall.   For a moment,

they stand upright, two stems suspended
on the water's surface.   I throw down my broom, reach out.

I can almost catch them, my own body departing
from itself, from the heartbreaking

miscalculations of a summer, a year, my arms thrust up
over the river, one last fling before sinking.

FAMILY REUNION

I am waiting in line, crazy with the deep south
smorgasbord delirium of chicken and biscuits and greens.

The kids go: you're it.
No you're it.
No you're it.
You are.
No you are.
Stop.

My cousin Sean goes out the back door with the trash.
Those furious bees in the rib sauce.

Tired old chain-link fence, the dog brings over a shoe.
Inside everyone is dying in increments.

My aunt mumbles out the window,
faggots ain't welcome here.   Sean draws a circle in the clay,

smacks his neck.   The dog rubs her ass on the concrete.
In the house a hot smell rises

from something old and slowly opening —
Horse flies, mesmerized, blow in.

MY NAMESAKE IS DYING

I have read, after the fourth session, you lose
your eyelashes and your nose hair.   I am 800 miles away,
driving past the world's largest steel peach.

All night on the midnight pixel
electric doodad highway
in the spit-cooked concrete heat

I am saying heavenly God,
I am saying heavenly God,
I cannot reach her from here.

Now I am driving past
the "Life is Short,
Eternity Isn't" billboard.

❧

Outside your house tonight,
the moon orphans all those stars.

In a halo of morphine, you watch me
swim in the old vinyl pool.

Like you did when I was three.
I open underwater, page turning.   Unbound,

the chapters float upward.   My hands,
those unwieldy nets, skim furiously.

❧

Next to your snow boots and the golf clubs
is the narc box.   The nurses buzz in and out
of the closet, mother-loaded needles in hand.

Teetering in the bathroom
with lipstick, you say to my mother:
Rose, get me a fly swatter

and (scooting the air from your face),
Shoo angels, shoo.

❧

I water your flowers, grass already dissecting
the neat beds you cleaned last summer.
I picture those hands mud-mooned and strong.
Such tired fingers now fumbling a spoon.
Beside the wine, my cousin stacks cans of Ensure.
My uncle skims the pool.
Towels exhale on a hinge of sun.
All day around your frail body, we work.
You breathe.   Miles away, the sea
weeds a million acres with only a sound.

❧

Let's pretend I don't exist
you cannot see me
stealing the unused Percocet
you cannot see me still floating
to the bottom of the pool

everyone inside addressing envelopes
or throwing out your old cigarettes
or labeling the neighbors' Tupperware
you cannot see me hiding a photo
in my suitcase, my uncle's only copy
of you in your father's tobacco field
wearing green overalls beside the red kilns
in August the plants behind
you rising yellow with sugar
the sweet yellow rising

Laws of Gravity

After your funeral
I fly over a great lake
of tiny songbirds, lubed up warblers
sunflower seed-full and heading south
from here, it seems, every direction — the same
as inside a glove box
where rivers stand upright,
drain-wise lugworms float upward
into the molder and stink of stack pipes,
shining celestial wakes
of garden snails
jet overhead.   For a moment
after loss, gravity is displaced, lessened
not for the living.   A man
carries his wife
across a pasture in a lard can —
suddenly her ashes sail skyward forever.   The birds
bury in the horse nettle, wingless.

LUCKY STARS

Thank the stars.   They expect nothing.   To survive the night
pinned up is something.   Dandelions tack to grass

even after fire.   My scars, uncluttered and blue.
The moles like nails.   Everything that holds

me here: two sisters in feet pajamas
pretend to have a picnic on shag carpet.

The father on the floor rolls towards them,
a bull dozer singing: vroom vroom vroom.

Digging in.   Mowed over and laughing.   Getting up
with static charged hair.   Moon pulling the hem of an ocean.

Shells unclasp.   Birds wildcat for crabs, yellow tongs
pulling.   Blue pincer legs ripped off,

the body swims forward.   What I did not expect to survive,
I've already forgotten.   Simmering stars grow bones

into the dark.   By morning, the sky serves thin soup.   To survive the day
so naked is something.

Thanks for a Great Season See You in the Spring

Bumper to bumper stars honk from their darkened
display cooler, that off-shore sky advertising

the dark and frozen shore where I've moved recently,
despite swearing off moving again,

my apartment among the boarded-up motor hotels
sitting beside the potluck sea noisily calling

anything corn-colored and vitamin-like into it —
the sun, the suet-fed, two fishing boats

go missing, the Tast-ee Freeze is for rent,
the wind drunk-dials absurdly, a kerfuffle

of cats and one folksinger rhyme by the True Value.
Everywhere, an inward propagation, the sea is

a white forest of lungs, the dunes grope obsessively
and recapture themselves.   I am touched deeply

by the RealFeel.   I hold hands with a stranger
through a wind advisory.

CHASING AFTER THE WIND

A wood pile
piling wood in the rain
and the dog barking at
the yellow school bus unloading
anyone in a hat makes her crazy
a man splitting wood
in his square foot of backyard
he's out there all day
like a brown tobacco stain
on a yellow beard you notice him.
Stop.   You are tired.
It is raining and a red leaf
just fell from the sky and don't you
piling wood taste how
the hours are heavier squash
shaped in the shortening days
of November.   Wait.
It is someone's birthday
and you are piling wood
in the rain now
the dog is under the porch steps
and the wood is barking
on your sweater
the dog has stopped and the leafing
is louder and you are getting tired
under the falling
something now piled high
ordering the moonlight into pickets
the dog is snapping at a leaf
you are getting tired splitting
the cold air a twig snaps

the moonlight in two
it is a birthday
and the rain is piling wood.
Stop.   You are tired.
The old screen door slams
in the peddling breeze
someone throws a bottle at the dog
beans float with fatback
you are carrying rain in
you are carrying in leaves
someone carries a wooden fist
the beans look heavy and the fire
behind the screen snaps
at the dog pedaling away
the door says Get us some wood
you open the screen the moon is
the neighbor's TV snaps the leaves
the door.   Look.
It is your birthday
says a word on your palm
this is living Pile the wood.

How the Mind Works

after Archimedes

The tenuous equilibrium
between, for example,
a small house and a backdoor
sea.   The fulcrum,
the boulder, a bullet
of soil shifts

in Las Colinas, the mudslides
green soccer fields lined with
mattresses, relief trucks
teetering with blankets,
tortillas, diapers, and toiletry
hinges

a mother removing a splinter,
two planes, two pressed fingers
and the dirty palm of a child,
his cry, an equal and opposite
reaction to relief or the possibility
of a wood shard festering

in the ooze of inertia
in contained spaces, in hospital wards,
in an airplane cabin —
a passenger's mind unbalanced,
the lithium level unchecked (or cocktails

cut-off) — fingernail clippers,
a dangerous weapon right
under the pivot point, the sidewise
file gripped, thrown toward

a tag of skin, the space of friction,
the brain is a lever:

Give me the place to stand,
and I shall move the earth.

Why the Chicken Never Crosses

Wind picks up the street.   Minutes bend
like a waist just before diving off.
It's always the same,

this gap between knowing
and what to do with knowing —
the elastic separation.

Leaves and wind.   Leaves and wind.
Fall is a verse and a verse and refrain.
(New song: frost.)

The first few downed leaves cross the street,
scratch and sound sideways
like ghost crabs.

I look down at my red sneakers, the laces undone.
How vulnerable is one knee on cement,
two fingers carefully pulling string.

What I learn is always taking off.
The street is like a clothesline:
shadows, milkweed unpin.

Tails

Sea-side jazz band wind and a slipknot of snow.
My mittens stiffen around a knotted blue bag.

Run and wait, run and wait —
paws on the trail.

I hum the only prayers I know, the same four words —
two white leaves flipping a coin on a hedge of wind:

Dear Lord?   Heads.
Thank you.   Tails.

When my sister asks if I am Saved,
I say yes, every once in a while I am.

Peanut shells skate across Long Pond.
A bright yellow leaf, veins still red,

shines under ice.
Tails on the trail.   Tails.

Onions

1.

Moving quietly in the neon light
you pull open flaps within flaps, spill white meat
onto the cutting board,

slicing onions for soup.
We talk about the sensitivity   of dark and light
eyes, yours waterless, solid as soil,

mine emptying as I watch
your lean arms, the engagement of gliding tendons,
the elbow holding its soft cup

of veins.   Forgive me for picturing
another life, the same blue crease gripping a needle
of junk, the flushing face,

the heavy, pink nod, the blood
suddenly floating   in free-fall   behind the weighted lap bar
of bones.   I roll back

my burning eyes.   From a distance,
it is beautiful, the field of limp green shoots   falling slowly
before their white hearts are lifted   from the mud.

2.

I love your fingertips
curled away from the knife,
the heart and palate   working together,

holding the onion tightly
to prevent crushing.
I do not remember my first.   In Georgia

my grandmother eating them like apples.
A history of onions: thin cells
leave little trace.   Cavities left in the soil

tell us more
of hardship.   The bare gums
of a farmer or addict, everyone in my family.

You understand why I cry here so far
north, settling, the days quickly flattening
against my ears, the collapsed eyes

of pumpkins everywhere.   To feel better, we watch
the Series, eat hot dogs with pickles
and onions.   In the South, fat Vidalias roll

on conveyor belts, their paper skins
blow from the empty crates like snow
my family never sees.   How seriously you take my blues

and cooking.   How your slicing
is a keyhole, a precise instrument opening —
on the other side,   a smaller, sharper light.

To the High School Prom Queen

There's just one highway.   The wind rears up like a circus beetle.
The setting sun hangs purple tags on the mountains

as if night were for sale too.   Las Vegas tilt o' wheels
its neon legs toward the desert —

humming seamstress of broke down and ritz
tacking embroidery floss and velvet swag on everything.

You are there, in the Women's Correctional Institute,
sleeping on a cot in a former storage closet.

Miles away, snow wriggles through dune and pine.
Pork chops thaw in my sink; potatoes boil on the stove.

You behind a bar-pull of stars, sky-wandering
and homeless without the concrete hooks of a city.

You on the streets, cash-wadded and meth-loaded.
You, knocking out someone's teeth.

Dear friend, I have finally stopped trying to kill myself.
Sometimes the light comes in tiny points,

shark-toothed and smaller than stars;
sometimes, it sprays over everything.

Every day my scars shrivel up — lids of rain
in a garbage can.   Once I wanted to travel.

Now I'm in love with the way whole Saturdays
weigh on my back with laminate flooring and wood piling.

My girlfriend and I throw chops on the grill,
fat floats above the trees.   Shaken,

sometimes the stars, the pine needles spiral gracefully.

LOVE SONG, SALT

A carrot bag of clams shimmers by the screen door
next to the swelling green flea shampoo.   I wash myself outdoors

in a spreading pool of Ivory soap freckled
with rusted Lady Bic stubble.   A pigtail of sweat rolls

down your face trying to shake the Krazy Jane's Mixed Salt
swollen like wet coals.   Orange meat strings unbraid

over a fire.   I left everything for this life.   My heart no longer empties
when forced indoors.   Sandwich crusts of beach

fall from my pockets.   You inflate a space even sitting quietly
in a waiting room of stubbed toes or in a bath sidelined

with tweezers, thin *Rosa Rugosa* prickers buried
in your soaked hands.   The knuckles

of spring bulbs unwrap in the basement.   Slowly everywhere
the shadow-cooling dugouts of sea grass expand, the pale organs

of striped throw-backs swim in a cooler awaiting transplant
like my heart did when it first tasted your invisible current.

HUMMING THE DOUBLEMINT SONG

What with *Dancing with the Stars* canceled,
we surf for a series on giant squid,
instead are hooked by a countdown

of celebrity meltdowns.   Outside, the snow,
blue roan and hoofbeating,
tromps gently through the pines.

Corn ruffles in the Whirley Pop,
your stove smoking with old shoot-outs
of onion and oil, small ignitions

of soup.   How we find ourselves
colliding, droplets on the half n' half,
cabinets expanding with nothing but salt and milk bones,

a pan of stew boiled over, a few pieces of dog kibble
doubling in the bottom of a water bowl,
creep deformation, a few viscous crumbs

of snow, bright purple eggs gumming
through sea water, a certified tentacle
of ink lassoing your name + my name, sticky jingles.

To a Clam

Some nights we both dream of teeth.
I wake from my noisy engine of sleep.
You wake from yours.
By morning, the marsh erases what is lost —

My teeth swim forward like minnows
caught in a Ziplock of breath.
Some nights I hear you chew your bright lips.
I think of white cabbage tacos

and also, of clams.
All evening the mudflats tongue at my window.
I want to throw back today's harvest,
all the living rocks in my pail.

Tonight, the sky drops another shiny molar.
The wedge-footed moon crawls for the sea.
I fall asleep and my crumbling words build islands.
Only you, with your hollow beak, can fly that far.

THOUGHT THINKING ITSELF

Suddenly, all the things I do not understand
discreetly twinkle below a surface.

A gristle of duckweed gleams through a thick chop of ice.
The green wafer of a fish drifts up through a pudding of eelgrass.

For ten years, I lived mostly on psych wards and nothing burnished more
than my overestimated connection to grief.

One year, my roommate consumed small amounts of arsenic for a week.
Everyday, she stirred it through her warm brown soup.

Three blood transfusions later, she lit two portable charcoal grills
in the back seat of her Subaru and died.

After a month on a psych ward, doctors discovered I had 15 personalities.
I was twenty.   I made them all up.   This is a true story.

We reassemble our lives and discover nothing.
Just under the skin, a tiny wick of green ignites a garlic clove.

In the early 1990s, something went terribly wrong.
All around me, young women were diagnosed and diagnosed.

If I could live my twenties again, I would not sever to untangle —
flight is a single ligament balanced between two forces.

In the snow, the geese link chains and I follow their past.
There is nothing at the end to unravel.

POMACE

Before breakfast, my father and I
eat the muscadines he grows
among the mountain laurel sprawl.

We break the purple skin with a tooth,
suck out the heart, spit the seeds.
I tell him I am better, stronger.

Finally on my own —
I have a bed frame, a desk lamp.
I have a small cherry book case.

Resurrection ferns gather our spit.
Cobweb lines hold the saplings straight.
My father is pale and small.

We walk slowly,
a seed rides his white beard
up the long hill home.

CONSIDER THE LILIES OF THE FIELD

Years ago I slept on the sidewalks
in the Tenderloin, a summer junkie
selling baking soda crack to college boys.
Every day the fog cribs in; the blue gum cypress
sleep underwater and I do not feel a drop.
I am thirty now.   Still Silva and Reggie use
their caked brown fingers all day twisting
baggies behind Miz Brown's Feed Bag.
Silva keeps her teeth in her scarf.
I write all day and into the violet night,
my heart soaked through —
all my life I've been vain in my grief.
Meanwhile, the thin-skinned lilies
hold more than their weight of water
deep in the perpetually shedding forest —
they toil not, neither do they spin.

ACKNOWLEDGMENTS

I am grateful to the following journals for publishing poems or versions of poems that appear in this manuscript:

The Adirondack Review: "Song for the Scars"
Black Warrior Review: "Thanks for a Great Season See You in the Spring"; reprinted in *Verse Daily*
Brick and Mortar Review: "How the Mind Works"
Cimarron Review: "Thought Thinking Itself"
Folio: "Jewelweed"
Hayden's Ferry: "To the High School Prom Queen"
The Iowa Review: "From the Motel-by-the-Hour"
Margie: "Silver Bimbo Mud Flap Song" and "Skimmers" (formerly "Jesus Bugs")
Phoebe: "Hiking the Appalachian Trail"
Shankpainter: "Shucking" and "To a Clam"
Southern Indiana Review: "My Namesake Is Dying"
The Sow's Ear Poetry Review: "Elsewhere"
Whiskey Island Review: "Halfway-to-Hell Club"

"Elsewhere," "Cat" (under the title "How the Heart, Too"), and a shorter version of "My Namesake Is Dying" received a 2008 Dorothy Sargent Rosenberg Poetry Prize.

I am deeply indebted to my family: Dad and Judy, Mom and Paul, and my sisters. Special thanks to Elizabeth Winston, Kim Addonizio, Susan Kan, Amy Dillard, Robert Youree, my friends at FAWC, Marie Howe, Gretchen Carswell, and to my former professors, Jennifer Atkinson, Eric Pankey and Susan Tichy. I am especially grateful for the George Mason Thesis Completion Fellowship and to The Fine Arts Work Center in Provincetown.

Nancy K. Pearson, originally from Chattanooga, Tennessee, received her MFA from George Mason University.   Recently, she completed two seven-month poetry fellowships at The Fine Arts Work Center in Provincetown.   An avid runner and cyclist, she now lives on Cape Cod with her partner.

About Perugia Press

Perugia Press publishes one collection of poetry each year, by a woman at the beginning of her publishing career. Our mission is to produce beautiful books that interest long-time readers of poetry and welcome those new to poetry. We also aim to celebrate and promote poetry whenever we can, and to keep the cultural discussion of poetry inclusive.

Also from Perugia Press:
- *Beg No Pardon*, by Lynne Thompson
- *Lamb*, Frannie Lindsay
- *The Disappearing Letters*, Carol Edelstein
- *Kettle Bottom*, Diane Gilliam Fisher
- *Seamless*, Linda Tomol Pennisi
- *Red*, Melanie Braverman
- *A Wound On Stone*, Faye George
- *The Work of Hands*, Catherine Anderson
- *Reach*, Janet E. Aalfs
- *Impulse to Fly*, Almitra David
- *Finding the Bear*, Gail Thomas

This book was typeset in Arno Pro, a type family designed in 2007 by Robert Slimbach for Adobe Systems, Inc. The type, both beautiful and legible, combines classical letterforms with a warm and graceful calligraphic style.